Simply Notetaking and Speedwriting

Simply Notetaking and Speedwriting

Learn How to Take Notes Simply and Effectively

Kristine Setting Clark

ROWMAN & LITTLEFIELD
Lanham • Boulder • New York • London

Published by Rowman & Littlefield
An imprint of The Rowman & Littlefield Publishing Group, Inc.
4501 Forbes Boulevard, Suite 200, Lanham, Maryland 20706
www.rowman.com

86-90 Paul Street, London EC2A 4NE, United Kingdom

Copyright © 2022 by Kristine Setting Clark

All rights reserved. No part of this book may be reproduced in any form or by any electronic or mechanical means, including information storage and retrieval systems, without written permission from the publisher, except by a reviewer who may quote passages in a review.

British Library Cataloguing in Publication Information Available

Library of Congress Cataloging-in-Publication Data

Names: Clark, Kristine Setting, 1950– author.
Title: Simply notetaking and speedwriting: learn how to take notes simply and effectively / Kristine Setting Clark.
Description: Lanham, Maryland: Rowman & Littlefield, 2022. | Includes bibliographical references. | Summary: "Simply Notetaking and Speedwriting will teach the student how to record notes in various formats and how to utilize notetaking when studying or reviewing for an exam"—Provided by publisher.
Identifiers: LCCN 2021037548 (print) | LCCN 2021037549 (ebook) | ISBN 9781475850871 (cloth) | ISBN 9781475850888 (paperback) | ISBN 9781475850895 (epub)
Subjects: LCSH: Note-taking—Handbooks, manuals, etc.
Classification: LCC LB2395.25 .C53 2022 (print) | LCC LB2395.25 (ebook) | DDC 371.30281—dc23
LC record available at https://lccn.loc.gov/2021037548
LC ebook record available at https://lccn.loc.gov/2021037549

Contents

Introduction		vii
1	The Importance of Notetaking	1
2	Speedwriting—A Shortcut to Notetaking—Common Abbreviations	3
3	Creating Your Own Personalized Notetaking System	9
4	A Prescription for Successful Notetaking	11
5	How to Focus	13
6	Look and Listen for the Clues	19
7	Practicing with a Recorded Presentation	25
8	How to Take Notes During a Lecture	27
9	Highlighting the Facts	29
10	When the Chapter Is Too Long	33
11	How to Take Notes During a News or Subject Interview	41
12	How to Take Notes During a Meeting and How to Take Minutes During a Meeting	43

| 13 | Compare, Contrast, and Lists | 49 |
| 14 | Test Yourself! | 57 |

Speedwriting Dictionary	65
References	105
About the Author	107

Introduction

Simply Notetaking and Speedwriting is a simple and effective notetaking program that is essential to student academic success. Notetaking is a major component in learning and understanding how to recognize and identify main ideas, key facts, and details.

Simply Notetaking and Speedwriting will also teach the student how to record notes in various formats and how to utilize notetaking when studying or reviewing for an exam. Worksheets and practices are included in many of the chapters.

What makes *Simply Notetaking and Speedwriting different* from other notetaking curriculums is that it teaches a form of *shorthand* to notetaking. For example, in chapters 2 and 3 the student will be taught how to utilize *speedwriting* when taking notes. They will also be guided through developing their own, personal *speedwriting* system. Included at the back of the book is an extensive, alphabetized catalog of *Commonly Used Words and Their Speedwriting Abbreviations*.

Taking effective notes, whether by hand or on a computer/tablet, helps the student to retain information on what has been said or written down long after the lecture or classroom lesson is over.

Whether you are taking notes from a book, for research, from a lecture, from a recording or from media/online resources, *Simply Notetaking and Speedwriting* will give you the tools to retain information and master the skill of notetaking.

Chapter 1

The Importance of Notetaking

The ability to take clear and comprehensive notes is vital to students' academic success. Good notetaking allows students to understand and learn course material for assignments and exams.

The following are four reasons for taking good notes.

(1) Notetaking helps you to pay attention. Your concentration will become better because you now have something specific to focus on. It also helps you to remember the ideas that you are writing down.
(2) What's important and what's not important will become easier for you to recognize.
(3) You will always have a permanent record of notes from the various lectures and chapters that you have read.
(4) By reviewing your notes regularly, you will be able to remember what you have read or heard. Notetaking also helps you to organize your ideas.

Now let's pretend that you are home alone. The phone rings, and it's for your brother, Brian. It's his baseball coach and he has a message for him that is very important. You ask the coach to hold on for a moment while you get paper and a pen. You ask the coach to speak slowly so that you can write down EVERY word.

Brian:

Practice has been changed. It will be at 3:30 at Lincoln High School instead of 4:00 at Washington High School.

If you had been skilled in notetaking, you may have written it like this:

Bri – Prac chngd fr Wash. @ 4 to Linc. @ 3:30

Instead of writing down each and every word of the phone message, all you would have needed to do was write down the main facts. The main facts are what allow your memory to remember what was said. This is what notetaking is all about.

Chapter 2

Speedwriting—A Shortcut to Notetaking—Common Abbreviations

Many students find it to their advantage to abbreviate certain words. It helps them to write faster and concentrate more on what they are reading or listening to. More often than not, some students create/invent their own notetaking abbreviations sometimes, without even knowing it.

When creating your own system of abbreviations watch out for the following:

(1) Be careful not to use the same abbreviation for more than one word if possible, but you should be able to identify the word according to the context in which it is used.
(2) You want to be able to easily read back what you have written down. To insure this, do not crowd your words as if you were writing a composition. Leave enough space between each word so that your notes will be clear and easy to read.
(3) Do not use periods when abbreviating. Periods are only used in place of the participle "ing." An example of this is the word "going." The shorthand version of "ing" is a period. In other words, you would write going like this: go.
(4) Use technical symbols such as: & (and), + (add, plus), − (less, minus), $ (dollars, money), % (percent), @ (at), ? (question), ! (to exclaim or show importance).

3

(5) Always use standard, English abbreviations. Here are a few examples:

care of	c/o
without	w/o
pound	Lb
ounce	Oz
height	Ht
weight	Wt

(6) Eliminate vowels whenever possible. Here's an example: *developed (dvlpd), individual (indv)*. For words ending in *ment*, draw a line (___). For example: *development (dvlp__)*. And as stated previously, use a period(.) for words ending in *"ing."* For example—*developing (dvlp.)*.

To become successful in your notetaking, you will need to memorize (remember) the symbols (abbreviations) that you have chosen to use. The whole idea of notetaking is to omit as many letters as possible and still be able to recognize the word. If the original word is long, it will be easier to recognize its abbreviation. If the original word is short, it will be easier to read back if you *leave in its vowels*.

Be sure not to make your abbreviations so short that you cannot recognize what you have just written. Remember if it takes longer to memorize a symbol than to write the entire word, find another symbol. Don't rush your notetaking. Be patient and learn only a few symbols and/or abbreviations per week.

To help you get started with your own system of abbreviations, here is a list of some of the most frequently used words and their abbreviations:

COMMONLY USED WORDS AND THEIR ABBREVIATIONS

A	
add (plus)	+
adjective	adj
adverb	adv
against	vs
America/American	Am
and	&
and so forth	etc
approximately	aprox
are	r
arrive	arriv
as soon as possible	asap
assignment	assg_____
at	@
B	
because	bec
before	bef
between	btw
book	bk
C	
chapter	ch
composition	comp
computers	compu
conjunction	conj
continue	cont
D	
decrease	dec
definition	def
democracy	dem
different	dif

E	
English	Eng
equals	=
example	ex
F	
finished	fin
for	4
fraction	frac
French	Fr
from	fr
G	
geography	geog
German	Gr
government	gov____
governor	govnr
H	
history	hist
homework	hmwk
I	
increase	inc
information	info
introduction	intro
L	
leave	lv
less than	<
library	lib
M	
maximum	max
memorize	mem
minimum	min

money	$
month	mo
more than	> |//
N	
nothing	0
noun	n
number	#
P	
page	pg
paragraph	p
percent	%
person	prsn
physical	phys
Physical Education	PE
possible	poss
preposition	prep
president	pres
principal/principle	prin
problem	prob
product	prod
pronoun	pr
Q	
question	?
R	
recognize	rec
reference	ref
regarding	rgrd.
S	
science	sci
sentence	sen
Spanish	Span

spelling	sp
study	stdy
T	
that	th
that is	i.e.
therefore	t/f
U	
United States of America	US/USA
V	
verb	v
W	
week	wk
which	wh
with	w/
without	w/o
woman	wmn
word	wd
Y	
year	yr
you	u

When writing out numbers, the following abbreviations may be used:

first, second, third, fourth 1st, 2nd, 3rd, 4th, (etc.)
one, two three, four, five 1, 2, 3, 4, 5, (etc.)
A more extensive list of abbreviations can be found in the back of the book.

Chapter 3

Creating Your Own Personalized Notetaking System

Use the following pages to write down your own, personal notetaking system. You can also use the abbreviations that you have previously learned in chapter 2; record words that are often used in your classes or that you, yourself, use often.

First, let's recap:

(1) Use as few letters as possible while still being able to recognize the word.
(2) Do not use the same abbreviation for more than one word.
(3) Do not abbreviate a word so much that you will not be able to recognize it later.
(4) After you have recorded your words and abbreviations, put them in alphabetical order so that it will be easier to find them when needed.

WORDS ABBREVIATIONS

Write the entire word on the top line and the abbreviation of that word on the second line.

_____
_____
_____

Be sure to keep your *Personal Notetaking System* handy at all times. It will serve as a reference for you. Every time you come up with a new abbreviation, record it in your personal system. Take time to review and study these abbreviations.

Chapter 4

A Prescription for Successful Notetaking

Want to take the *work* out of homework? Learn to take better notes in class!
When going over your notes, do you sometimes have trouble understanding what you have just written? Does it look like another language of some sort? Then, here's a prescription for successful notetaking.
The key to taking good notes is *PAYING ATTENTION*. During a lecture you should:

Listen,
Concentrate,
Think,
and then, Write.

Always have your computer or notebook open and a pencil or pen in your hand so you will be ready to write.
The following is a list to help you on your way to successful notetaking:

1. If taking notes by hand, always have a good supply of paper in your binder. Use a full size sheet, not small pieces of paper.
2. Always have blue and/or black pens in your pencil/pen case (inside your binder).

3. Always use a new sheet of paper or a blank document in your computer for each lecture. This way you won't mix up which notes go with which lecture/subject. Note: Keep your computer subject files separate.
4. Make sure that your writing or printing (whichever is easiest for you) is clear enough to be read later.
5. Use only abbreviations and symbols that you will understand and recognize. Don't start using new symbols and/or abbreviations because you may forget what they mean.
6. Be sure to include the date and the subject (topic) of each lecture at the top of the page. Don't forget to number each page.
7. Keep each individual subject's notes together in your binder or in separate file on your computer.
8. When taking notes, skip lines only when the idea or fact changes.
9. Keep margins for writing down *side notations*. This will keep your main notes from becoming cluttered.
10. Don't take time to erase, just draw "one" line through the incorrect word and write the correct word next to it.
11. *Definitions* and *formulas* should be copied exactly as you hear or see them.
12. Write main ideas, facts, and key words only—never sentences!
13. Never use articles: a, an, the. They are not important when you are taking notes.
14. To help you remember the *important* words, you can underline, circle, asterisk (*), or use highlighting markers.
15. If you didn't get all of the lecture, leave some space on your paper to be filled in later. Check with the teacher or another student for the missed information.
16. Focus your mind on the central idea(s).

Notetaking is not just for classroom lectures. It is just as important when recording facts from a textbook.

Chapter 5

How to Focus

In chapter 4 you learned that the key to good notetaking is paying attention. During a lecture or while studying, you should always do the following:

Listen or Read
Concentrate
Think
and then, Write

Notetaking will become easier and easier when you know what to listen/look for. Here are some helpful tips on helping you to focus.

LISTEN to or READ the title.
CONCENTRATE on what it says or means.
THINK of a question or two relating to that specific title.
WRITE that question or questions down. As you listen or read on, look for the answers to your questions.

The following are the questions (where applicable) you will ask yourself:

Who
What
When
Where
Why
How

Read the following title and use the above tips to help you decide which questions to ask. Remember, not all questions will apply all the time.

THE 1989 SAN FRANCISCO EARTHQUAKE

Your first (or main) question would probably be: WHAT happened during the 1989 quake and WHY/HOW did it happen? Now you can begin to FOCUS on learning.

What
Why
How

Now let's look at another title:

THE BEST CANDIDATES FOR THE PRESIDENCY

WHO are the best candidates for the Presidency and WHY and HOW were they chosen?

Who
Why
How

Now you are ready to put to work what you have just learned.

How to Focus

Fill in the blank or blanks by asking one or more questions relating to the following titles. Remember, not all questions will apply.

FOOTBALL'S GREATEST QUARTERBACK

Who
What
When
Where
Why
How

HURRICANE LEAVES HUNDREDS HOMELESS

Who
What
When
Where
Why
How

CONTROLLING STRESS

Who
What
When
Where
Why
How

HOTTEST TEMPERATURE EVER RECORDED

Who
What
When
Where
Why
How

PLANE CRASHES AFTER TAKEOFF

Who
What
When
Where
Why
How

DOG SAVES CHILD IN SWIMMING POOL

Who
What
When
Where
Why
How

CAUSE OF FIVE ALARM FIRE

Who
What
When
Where
Why
How

"VOLCANO ERUPTS IN HAWAII"

Who
What
When
Where
Why
How

NEW VACCINE DISCOVERED

Who
What
When
Where
Why
How

Teacher's Note: After the class has completed the assignment, have them contrast and compare the answers they chose.

Chapter 6

Look and Listen for the Clues

Recording Only the Important Facts and Ideas

There are four main criteria (requirements) for determining whether or not something is worthy of notetaking. These main criteria are as follows:

Category/Subject
Relevance/Relating to
Importance
Personal Bias/Your Opinion

When reading a book or listening to a lecture, you should be considering all four of the criteria.

Let's begin reviewing each of these criteria. We'll start with *Category*.

The *Category* tells you what type of information it is. Here are a few examples of categories:

Large American Cities
Famous Mystery Writers
Top 10 Colleges in America

Chapter 6

Any and all information is divided into two basic categories. They are *Facts* and *Opinions*. Be sure not to confuse one with the other. They are both very different. Here are the reasons why.

A *Fact* is and will always be a *true statement*. The key word here is *true*.

Example: The sun rises in the east and settles in the west.

The majority of the facts that you will be taking notes on have been established by *Evidence*. The definition of evidence is: To show *proof* that someone or something is *true*. This can be related to the following:

Scientific Research backs up its information with fact through carefully conducted scientific experiments. An *Authority (an accepted source of information)*, such as a teacher or scientist or a professional in his or her known field, is a *source of fact*.

Example: Astronomers discovered that there are nine planets in our solar system. They are Mercury, Venus, Earth, Mars, Jupiter, Saturn, Uranus, Neptune, and Pluto.

When you have several or more *reliable/reputable* sources that report something as fact, you can sometimes cite the sources but *be careful*. Again, it depends on *who* is reporting and *what* they are reporting on.

Example: According to Jacques Cousteau, oceanographer and explorer, we should respect the ocean as we respect the earth.

Opinion can be anything that a person or persons believe *in without showing evidence or fact. Never* rely on opinions!

Example: "I believe that there is human life on other planets."

Where is *the fact or evidence here? Unless it can be proven that* there is human life on other planets, the above statement will remain an *opinion*.

The following are some examples of the differences between FACT and OPINION:

LARGE AMERICAN CITIES

Fact: San Francisco is a city in the state of California.
Opinion: San Francisco is the most beautiful city in the state of California.

FAMOUS MYSTERY WRITERS

Fact: Agatha Christie has written many mystery books.
Opinion: Agatha Christie is the world's greatest mystery writer.

AMERICAN COLLEGES

Fact: Notre Dame is located in South Bend, Indiana.
Opinion: I feel that Notre Dame is the best college in America.

When reading a book or listening to a lecture, look for the *clues* that signal *opinion*. Words like: *maybe, could be, possibly, and perhaps*, are selected words that state *opinion* and *not fact*.

Relevance is when the information you have been given relates to the topic you are writing about.

Be sure to write down the *main topic* of a lecture or reading assignment *before you begin taking notes*. This way you will be able to *identify which ideas are relevant and which are not*.

EXAMPLES OF RELEVANCE

Category: National Football League Quarterbacks
Topic: Jim Brown
Related Information: Jim Brown was an outstanding fullback for the Cleveland Browns during the 1957 to 1965.
Relevance: Brown led the NFL in rushing eight of his nine seasons with Cleveland and was inducted into the Pro Football Hall of Fame in 1971.

What *is* important and what *isn't*?

If a statement *isn't true*, it usually *isn't important*. It is only important if it *is related* to the topic. For example:

According to Christopher Columbus, the earth was flat.
We are not saying that the world was flat but that Columbus, himself, *believed* that the world was flat.
If you find that the *source* of the statement *is not reliable,* then the *statement is not important.*

Sometimes you may feel that certain information is important whereas others may not. That is your own *personal bias* and you have every right to jot down this information. *Note*: In parenthesis (), write down why you chose to add this information to your notes.

EXAMPLE OF PERSONAL BIAS

Fact: There are two Disney theme parks in the United States. One is located in Anaheim, California, and the other is in Orlando, Florida.
Personal Bias: After visiting both theme parks, I personally feel that Disneyland in Anaheim, California, is the better of the two.

When *listening* to a lecture, you will hear the speaker emphasize or stress certain words. These words are *clues* as to what is important. There are many *expressions* that a speaker will use. Throughout their lecture. Here are a few of the more commonly used *speech patterns*.

"Let's go over this again"
"This is of major importance"
"Because of this . . ."
"Don't forget this"
"What does this mean?"
"Listen carefully"

"The statistics show. . ."

"The result of this is . . ."
"Next . . ."

"The first is . . ."
"It is imperative that . . ."
"Remember this . . ."
"There are several reasons why . . ."

The more you listen to the speaker, the more you will begin to recognize a pattern of words that he or she uses.

Words such as *to summarize, therefore, and as follows* are *clues* that tell you that the following information is *important* and should be written down. It is very important to pay attention as to *how* the material is presented. See below:

1. *Listen for the change in voice tone*: Your teacher may speak more softly, more loudly, or more slowly. Be aware of words and/or phrases that are *stressed and/or repeated.* This is called *cuing.*
2. *Be aware of body language.* The pointing of a finger or the clenching of a fist, the grimacing of the face, or the squinting of the eyes.

The easiest part of a lecture is when the teacher *writing down the information* on the board or uses a computer or power point presentation. The major points are already written down for you.

Remember, all teachers lecture differently. All have different body language and voice tones. Get to know their various traits (habits or characteristics) and adjust your notetaking to their individual styles.

The following pages are worksheets for you to complete. Follow along with your teacher as she reads the instructions to you.

Worksheets

1. Write down three categories:
   1._____
   2._____
   3._____

2. Now write down one *fact* and one *opinion* about each of the categories you wrote down:

   Category 1:

   Fact:_____
   Opinion:_____

   Category 2:

   Fact:_____
   Opinion:_____

   Category 3:

   Fact:_____
   Opinion:_____

3. Next, choose *one* of the above three categories and write down *topic-related information* about that topic and something that is *relevant* to the topic and/or related information:

   Topic:_____
   Related Information: _____
   Relevant Information: _____

4. Give an example of *personal bias* from the above *topic* that you have chosen:

   Fact:_____
   Personal Bias: _____

Chapter 7

Practicing with a Recorded Presentation

Before we begin,
Never substitute the use of a recording device for notetaking when you can take the notes yourself. First of all, they are unreliable and basically, they are a waste of time. It is much easier to find out what's important by *watching* the lecture's expressions and other body language instead of just *listening* to a recording. Also, too much time is spent on replaying the recording over and over again. Your memory will regain more of the given information if you take the time to write it down.

You can, however, *benefit* from *practicing* with a recorder. The information you are about to read is designed to help you to improve your notetaking skills:

1. Practice listening to a recording so that you will have a chance to increase your notetaking skills. A good way of doing this is to read into the recorder a section of the chapter that you have been assigned for homework. This will work in two ways. First, you will be reading out loud the material that you need to study. Second, you will be practicing your notetaking skills.
2. As you speak into the device, pretend that you are the teacher lecturing to your class. Be sure to read each and every word as it is written. Change the tone of your voice and be sure to stress the

words and facts that you feel are *important*. Remember not to speak too fast. Slow down when you see a *comma*, stress all *underlined and italicized* words and stop at a *period.* Concentrate on the words that you are reading. After you have finished, rewind the recording and play it back. While listening to *your* lecture, take notes. You will be surprised at how much information your memory will recall. Remember, the *main idea* behind notetaking is to be able to *read it back!*

Teacher's Note: This exercise is ideal for use in a computer center. If the center is not available, use a recorder in your classroom and let the entire class perform the exercise together. In this case, individual students may read into the recorder or you, the teacher, can be the sole lecturer.

Chapter 8

How to Take Notes During a Lecture

Taking clear, comprehensive notes during a lecture is a challenge in itself. Not only must you be able to recognize what is noteworthy and what isn't but you must also be able to organize it in a clear and comprehensive manner. You must constantly focus all your attention on the speaker's *words* and *actions*. Remember, unlike a textbook, you seldom get a second chance to review what the speaker has said.

This chapter will help you to focus and organize yourself *before* and *during* a lecture. The following is a helpful format for you to follow:

First of all, you will need to prepare and get organized. Read any suggested texts and review your notes from previous lectures on the subject matter. This will help you to organize the material and see an overall picture of the subject. Some teachers hand out a course syllabus at the beginning of the semester. Keep this outline on *page one* of your course notes. Your notes should follow (in chronological order) the course outline. Each time you attend a lecture, look at the outline and *check off* the topic that was covered in the previous lecture. Briefly *review* these notes so you will be ready for the next topic to be discussed.

Arrive on time and be sure to have all the tools you will need ready to take notes. If you don't you will already be behind before the speaker even says one word. Be sure that your pens are working or your computer is ready to go.

The most difficult job in any lecture class is to give 100 percent of your attention to the speaker. Here are a few tips on how to keep your mind on the lecture.

1. Choose a seat in either the first or second row in the middle of the room. This will help you to see and hear the instructor. Being right in front of the teacher will also help you to stay awake and focused.
2. Don't sit next to your friends. They will do you more harm than good.
3. Be sure to get enough sleep the night before and eat a nutritious breakfast.
4. Remember that all teachers lecture differently. All have different body language, voice tone and various traits. Adjust your notetaking to their individual styles.
5. Don't be afraid to ask questions. If something isn't clear to you, ask for it to be explained.
6. Write only what's important. Not everything in a lecture will be significant. You don't need to write down *every* word or detail. Concentrate on writing down the main points and sub headings in your own words. If you miss anything, leave a blank space beneath the point in question and leave a question mark in the margin to remind you to review that point at a later time.
7. Make sure that your notes are *organized*. Your notes don't have to be perfect but they *do* need to be readable and organized if you expect to be able to read them in the future. Develop a system of highlighting headings and subtitles. Use bullets points, underlining, and indenting that make sense to you and stay with that same process from lecture to lecture. Be consistent with your speedwriting system. Do not write too much on one page. Also, don't write so small that you can't decipher what you have written. When using a computer, double space so your topics and sub-topics don't run together. Be sure to use diagrams or charts if they help you to make sense of your ideas.
8. Re-read your notes prior to your next class. It will help to reinforce your learning and understanding of the subject matter.

Chapter 9

Highlighting the Facts

In order to recognize main topics, ideas, or key words, you need to *highlight* them in one form or another. Highlighting is a quick and easy method of note taking from a text. It answers the who, what, when, where, why, and how by just marking the word or phrase.

One of the most useful tools in notetaking is the use of a highlighting pen. When key words and ideas are highlighted, it makes it easier for you to recognize them because they stand out from the rest of your notes.

Other forms of highlighting are to underline, circle, or *asterisk/star* certain words and/or phrases. When reading a book, you can make *notations (a brief note, sign or symbol)* in the margin of the book. Be sure to use only a pencil so it can be erased at a later time.

When using your computer/tablet, incorporate the underline, bold, asterisk*, and *italics* icons.

Read the example below on Great White Sharks and review some of the various forms of highlighting that are used.

GREAT WHITE SHARKS

Great shite sharks can be found throughout the world's oceans. They prefer cool water and stay close to the coast.

These fish are the largest predators on Earth and average 15 feet in length but some great whites have been measured at over 19 feet.

Great white sharks are grey with a white underbelly. The underbelly is where they get their name. Their body is streamlined and their tails can propel them through the water at a rate of 36 miles per hour. The mouth of the shark houses 300 sharp, triangular teeth arranged in several rows.

When sharks are young, they prey on small fish and sting rays. As they become older, they prey on sea lions, seals, and small whales.

The great white's sense of smell is incredible. They can detect seals two miles away and can smell a drop of blood within 25 gallons of water.

When great whites give birth, they usually have two to ten *pups*. From the moment of birth, she shows no care for her babies. As a matter of fact, the newborns immediately take care of themselves and swim off into the ocean.

Great whites have one predator and it is the killer whale.

Now let's go over the questions that apply to the above story on the Great White Sharks. Remember, not all questions will apply.

Who are you talking about? Great white shark, largest predator on Earth, 15 to over 19 feet long.

What makes them different from other fish? Grey with a white underbelly, have 300 sharp, triangular teeth and can travel 36 miles per hour. Eat sea lions, seals, and small whales. Have great sense of smell. Give birth to two to ten pups. Pups on their own from birth. Killer whale is their only predator.

Where are they found? Throughout the oceans. Like cool water and close to coast.

With the information from above, you can use the various highlighting tools to highlight the facts below.

Highlighting Pen

Great white sharks can be found throughout the world's oceans. They prefer cool water and stay close to the coast.

These fish are the largest predators on Earth and average 15 feet in length but some great whites have been measured at over 19 feet.

Underlining

Great white sharks are grey with a white underbelly. The <u>underbelly is where they get their name</u>. Their <u>body</u> is <u>streamlined</u> and <u>their tails</u>

can propel them through the water at a rate of 36 miles per hour. The mouth of the shark houses 300 sharp, triangular teeth arranged in several rows.

Asterisk/Star*

When sharks are young*, they prey on small fish* and sting rays.* As they become older*, they prey on sea lions,* seals*, and small whales.*

The great white's sense of smell* is incredible. They can detect seals two miles away* and can smell a drop of blood* within 25 gallons of water. *

Circle

When great whites give birth, they usually have two to ten pups. From the moment of birth, she shows no care for her babies. As a matter of fact, the newborns immediately take care of themselves and swim off into the ocean.

Great whites have one predator and it is the killer whale.

Now, read the story about *The Octopus*. In your notebook or on your computer, use a highlighting method above that best suits you.

THE OCTOPUS

No discussion of shy, underwater creatures is complete without some mention of the bashful octopus. It is most active at night, preferring to remain safe inside its lair during the daylight hours.

The octopus has eight tentacles lined with powerful suction cups which he uses to scramble across the bottom and to catch food. The catch, usually crab or lobster, is encircled by the tentacles and held securely by the suction cups, while the octopus separates the meat with sharp pecks of a parrot-like beak set around its mouth. The bite of the beak is poisonous and at times can be fatal. The smart scuba diver will confine his octopus activity to observation and photography.

The octopus is a swift swimmer. It jets itself through the water by drawing water into the muscular mantle that covers its body. It then ejects the water forcefully through a siphon.

Chapter 10
When the Chapter Is Too Long

Approaching a long chapter can be very discouraging. Some students may have difficulty deciding on what is important enough to take notes on and what isn't. One of the key factors in assigned reading is that it should be read differently from reading for pleasure. Here's how:

Know what to look for
Know what to *skim*
Know when to read every word

SKIMMING

Skimming is a quick way to look over the material you are about to read. It assists you in finding answers to specific questions. A form of skimming is called *pacing*.

Pacing will increase your reading and skimming speed. To do this, you move your hand down the page at a steady pace. This forces your eyes to speed up to the same pace and allows you to read large sections of words instead of reading word for word. Remember to use the *chapter breakdown* (found in the Table of Contents or throughout the chapter in the form of *bold titles/headings and/or subtitles* and/or *italicized* words). This will give you an idea about the *topic* and/or when the *topic has changed*. Again, important ideas are also usually in *bold* or *italicized* print.

Before you take on the task of taking notes on the entire chapter, you will first need to get a feeling of the chapter, itself. Start by:

READING the introduction
SKIMMING over the bold and italicized print, pictures, maps, charts, graphs, stats, etc.

Be sure to only concentrate on one section or paragraph at a time. This will make it easier for you to understand what you are reading and it will give you a better feeling as to what is important.

The textbook, itself, can also be of help to you. Most textbooks are broken down into chapters. Within these chapters you will find an *introduction* which is usually a pretty good breakdown of the chapter, *bold*, or *italicized* print, pictures (usually with captions), maps, charts, graphs, stats and more. A great deal of your notes will be taken from this breakdown.

Sometimes the author will write important questions at the *end of each chapter*. Be sure to read these questions *prior* to taking on the text. This will help you in what to look for when taking notes.

The following is a breakdown on how to take notes on an assigned reading:

LOOKING OVER YOUR TEXTBOOK

When opening your text look at the *Table of Contents*. What does it tell you or doesn't tell you? Does the book have an *index*? Does it have a section at the end of the text with *test question, charts, diagrams,* etc.? Are there any *summaries*? If so, read them through but only *after* you have *skimmed* through all of the pages. Be sure to look over the *introduction*. It can be extremely helpful as well as useful. Check to see how many *pages* the chapter contains. This will give you an idea of how long it will take you to *skim read* each one.

By seeing how the book is arranged, your chapter-by-chapter reading speed will increase.

In your binder, notebook or computer, write down/type what you feel is important or questions you may have. Be sure to write down the page number and paragraph of these facts and questions.

Once you have skimmed through the entire assigned reading, go back to the sections that you have questions about. Sometimes you will understand these sections better *after* you have completed the readings.

Now that you have had the opportunity to learn and absorb all of the above information, we are going to incorporate that knowledge into one of the best notetaking methods for taking on a long chapter: *outlining*.

OUTLINING

Outlining is a more structured and formal method of notetaking. If should list, in a logical and orderly manner, everything that you want or need to include in your paper. These ideas should be brief and show relative importance. Some typical uses of outlining might be an essay, a term paper, a book review or a speech. A good outline will help you to get your facts and ideas straight before you begin to write your paper.

Reading a chapter from beginning to end can result in a sea of facts, figures, and details. Sometimes the main ideas get overlooked because there is so much material to digest. By creating an outline, you allow yourself to sift through the information efficiently and effectively while focusing on what's important.

A well put together outline will serve as a study guide for exams, recall, and reference. If written correctly, you won't need to refer to your text. Outlining allows your brain to retain more information.

OUTLINES ARE MADE UP OF MAIN TITLES, SUBTITLES, AND DETAILS

The main titles should be of a general subject and start with a Roman numeral (I, II, III, etc.). The first word should be capitalized.

Subtitles must be closely related to the main title. Subtitles are indented and the first word is always capitalized.

Details must be closely related to the subtitles. They, too, are indented and capitalized but are identified with Arabic numerals (1, 2, 3, etc.), not Roman numerals. For even more detailed information regarding the subtitle indent under the Arabic numerals and use the lower case letters (a., b., c., etc.). (See example below entitled "Basic Outline Format").

BASIC OUTLINE FORMAT

I. Main Title
   A. Subtitle to Main Title
   B. Subtitle to Main Title
      1. Subtitle details to B
      2. Subtitle details to B
         a. Subtitle detail to 2
         b. Subtitle detail to 2
II. Main Title
   A. Subtitle to Main Title
   B. Subtitle to Main Title
   C. Subtitle to Main Title
III. Main Title

It is up to the writer to decide on how many main titles and subtitles adequately describe the subject. But there are some basic rules that must be followed when writing an outline. For every I there must be a II. For every A there must be a B. For every 1 there must be a 2 and for every a there must be a b.

Also be sure to line up the periods not the Roman numerals. Refer to above outline examples.

Before you begin your outline, follow these simple steps:

BEGIN WITH THE FIRST PARAGRAPH

In the first paragraph of the chapter, the author will set the stage regarding the topic of the chapter. You will be given a summation of the material that will be covered within the chapter. Sometimes the author will ask questions that will be answered during further readings. Don't forget to take your time reading this material as it is the basis of the chapter.

NOW SKIP TO THE LAST PARAGRAPH OF THE CHAPTER

By skipping to the last paragraph of the chapter you will read the author's summation of what the chapter was all about. At this time, you may even find answers to the previously asked questions you had from the first paragraph of the chapter. Again, take your time when reading.

RECORDING EACH AND EVERY MAIN TITLE

Now let's return to the first paragraph. Begin writing down each and every main title throughout the chapter. These can be easily found as they are usually in big, bold capital letters. They identify the topic of the material you are about to read. Be sure to leave three to four spaces for subtitles more, if needed.

NOW RECORD EACH AND EVERY SUBTITLE

Once you have completed writing down all of the main titles of the chapter, return to the beginning (of said chapter) and start writing down each of the subtitles that correspond with each of the main titles. Subtitles describe the main points of each of the main titles throughout the chapter.

TAKING NOTES—READING THE FIRST AND LAST PARAGRAPH OF EACH SUBTITLE SECTION

You will find the most important content of each subtitle section within the first and last paragraphs of that section. Your notes can range from a few words to complete sentences. Use whatever works best for you.

SKIM THE ENTIRE CHAPTER

Skim through the entire chapter and look for words in bold type or *italicized*. You may want to record these words and statements within your outline.

The following is an example of how your outline should look. The title should be the name of your chapter. Use Roman numerals (I. II. III.) for each main title and capital letters, A., B., C. for your subtitles. Arabic numbers (1. 2.) should be used for notes on each subtitle. And if there needs to be even more detailed, use a, b, and c.

SAMPLE OUTLINE

Chapter Title: The College Application Process

I. Choose Desired Colleges
   A. Visit and evaluate college campuses
   B. Visit and evaluate college websites
      1. Look for interesting classes
      2. Note important statistics

II. Prepare Application
   A. Write personal statement
      1. Choose interesting topics
         a. Describe an influential person in your life
           (1) Favorite high school teacher
           (2) Grandparents
         b. Describe a challenging life event
      2. Include important personal details
         a. Volunteer work
         b. Participation in varsity sports
   B. Revise personal statement

III. Complete Resume
   A. List relevant coursework
   B. List work experience
   C. List volunteer experience
      1. Tutor at foreign language
      2. Counselor for suicide prevention

Now you will have the opportunity to see how well you have absorbed the information on creating an outline. Read the following story about The Civil War and using all the tools you have learned outline the story in a clear and concise notetaking manner. Begin with outlining the story year by year. It will be easier for you to comprehend the material and not so intimidating.

THE CIVIL WAR

In the 1860s the northern and southern parts of the United States fought the American Civil War. The war started after eleven Southern states separated themselves from the United States and formed their own government. Their army fought the forces of the U.S. government. The Civil War/War between the states threatened to break up the United States.

The North and the South had been divided for many years over the issue of slavery. The Southern economy was based largely on cotton which was grown on large farms/plantations. Slaves did the majority of the work on these plantations. The Northern economy relied more on manufacturing, had small farms and used paid workers. Neither side wanted the other's ideas to spread to new states being created in the West. Northerners wanted to stop the spread of slavery. But Southerners believed that the U.S. government did not have the right to decide whether or not slavery should be allowed in a state. They feared that the government's next step would be to stop slavery altogether.

Southerners became more upset when Abraham Lincoln was elected in 1860 as the sixteenth president of the United States. Lincoln belonged to the Republican Party which opposed slavery. Southern states decided to secede/withdraw from the United States to protect their right to keep slaves. South Carolina, Mississippi, Florida, Alabama, Georgia, Louisiana, Texas, Virginia, Arkansas, North Carolina, and Tennessee seceded. They formed their own government and called it the Confederate States of the Confederacy. Jefferson Davis was the Confederate president.

The Northern states that stayed loyal to the United States were called the union. Four states—Kentucky, Missouri, Maryland, and Delaware stayed in the Union even though they allowed slavery. They were called border states. The western counties of Virginia refused to join the Confederacy. They later joined the Union as the state of West Virginia.

Going into the war the Union had several advantages over the Confederacy. They had more people, more industry, and more railroads. The Confederacy had stronger military leaders.

The American Civil War began on April 12, 1861, in Charleston, South Carolina. Confederate troops captured Fort Sumter from the Union Army.

1862

In 1862 Union forces had some success in the West. In February, Union troops Under General Ulysses S. Grant captured Confederate forts in western Tennessee. In April, Grant led the Union to victory in the Battle of Shiloh.

General Robert E. Lee led the Confederacy to important victories in the East. In August of 1862 his forces won a second battle at Bull Run. Next Lee invaded the North. Union troops stopped the Confederates at Antietam Creek, Maryland in September.

In December Lee's troops defeated a Union army at Fredericksburg, Virginia.

1863

At the start of the war President Lincoln wanted mainly to keep the United States together. Ending slavery was not his main goal. This changed after the Battle of Antietam. The Union victory encouraged Lincoln to issue a statement called the Emancipation Proclamation. This proclamation freed all enslaved people in Confederate states. As a result of the proclamation, many Blacks joined the Union army.

In May 1863, Lee defeated Union forces near Chancellorsville, Virginia but in July of that same year he suffered his first big defeat at Gettysburg, Pennsylvania.

The Battle of Gettysburg was the turning point of the war and favored the Union. The following day Grant captured Vicksburg, Mississippi. The Union now controlled the entire Mississippi River. In November 1863, Grant and General Sherman drove the Confederates out of Chattanooga, Tennessee.

1874–1865

In March of 1864, Grant was given full command of the Union army by Lincoln. While Grant fought in Virginia in September, Sherman was marching his way through Georgia and in December of 1864 captured Atlanta. He continued to march to the port city of Savannah located on the Atlantic Ocean. Sherman completed his mission by destroying all railroads and supply depots.

By March of 1865, Lee army was short on men and supplies. On April 3, Grant captured Richmond, Virginia, the Confederate capital.

On April 9, 1865, at Appomattox Court House in Virginia, Lee surrendered to Grant. The Union army was victorious and the country's bloodiest conflict had finally ended.

Chapter 11

How to Take Notes During a News or Subject Interview

Even in this day and age of super technology, a reporter's notebook and pen are still his or her best tools. Recorders are great for accurately capturing each and every quote but it can take too long to transcribe when you are constantly rewinding and replaying the device. This is especially true when you are on a deadline.

Many rookie reporters feel that the recorder captures every word, something that notetaking skills cannot. But if you incorporate your speedwriting skills you will only need your recorder to verify what you have taken down in notes. Read and incorporate the following tips on how to take good notes during a news or subject interview.

Every time you have the opportunity to record an interview, be sure to back it up with notes in your notebook. Remember, technology can fail.

Look professional! Learn all you can about your subject *prior* to your interview. Being prepared is key to doing a good job.

Generate a list of questions in the order in which you want to ask them. If possible, save the harder questions for the end as their responses will most likely take more time to answer.

Because interviews don't always go as planned, it's OK if the questions go into different directions. The main goal here is to *listen*. Be sure to let the subject know that their words are important to you. Nod your head to let the person know you understand them, maintain eye contact, lean forward toward them and take notes.

Key words and phrases are imperative! Be sure to write them down in your notebook. This is what you will be looking for when you are ready to write your story.

Sometimes the subject will speak too fast. Feel confident to request that they slow down so that you can catch up. Don't be afraid to have them repeat or clarify statements. Remember to annotate your notes with a star or asterisk. This will designate the most important parts of the interview as well as notating where a quote or statement should appear when writing your story. Example: If you have a quote that you would like to use at the beginning of the story, you may want to mark it with: Use in first para.

Upon completion of your interview. Review your notes immediately if possible. Be sure to transcribe them either in your notebook or computer so you can refer to them easily. Don't forget to *highlight* the main points and quotes that you will most likely use in your story.

Listening is very important in an interview but so is body language, expression, and tone of voice. Be sure to write down what you see as well.

We all have to take the good with the bad so at all times, be professional. Yes, there will be interviews that are difficult to deal with but get a feel for your subject and work around it the best you can.

Be sure to arrive early so you can review your surroundings. Be sure to be one of the last to leave so you will have time to review your notes and gather your thoughts.

If there is anything you have missed or were unclear about, be sure to contact your source and have that person clarify the problem.

Remember, take your time and ask only one question at a time. Don't be in a hurry and don't anticipate answers. Let the interviewee respond at their own pace. Don't interrupt. This is the quickest way to lose the interview. And whether or not you agree or disagree with them, don't wear your feelings on your sleeve. In other words, keep the tone of your voice neutral and calm and no facial contortions. You will get through the interview with much more ease.

Chapter 12

How to Take Notes During a Meeting and How to Take Minutes During a Meeting

Taking notes at a meeting demonstrates that you are paying attention. It also helps you to retain the information discussed and easily refer back to later. In this chapter you will learn tips on how to take efficient notes during a meeting.

The first thing you will need to do is decide whether you are taking *meeting notes* or *meeting minutes*. Though they both summarize the major points of the meeting, they are not the same.

MEETING NOTES

Meeting notes refer to basic facts. These facts include ideas, data, goals, deadlines, and any other important points that are covered in your meeting. Meeting notes can be quickly referenced.

TAKING EFFECTIVE MEETING NOTES

Meeting notes should be kept as simple but at the same time, allowing for important details. This is an excellent time to use your speedwriting skills.

There are three main points to be aware of when taking meeting notes:

| Main Points on the Agenda |
| Action Items |
| Ideas/Questions/Follow-Ups |

MAIN POINTS ON THE AGENDA

Record a short summation of each of the items listed on the agenda. Be sure not to forget to add the outcomes of the discussions. Limit each point to three sentences and be sure to verify any decisions or plans prior to writing your summation.

ACTION ITEMS

Immediately following a proposed action item, be sure to write down the assignment, who the assignment is assigned to and the due date.

IDEAS, QUESTIONS, AND FOLLOW-UPS

If you find that you have an idea, a question or a follow up after the meeting has been adjourned, be sure to include a section in your notes to jot down your thoughts. This will ensure that you don't forget what they were.

The following is a sample meeting notes template that you may want to use for your next meeting. You can revise this template to meet the needs of your meeting.

SAMPLE MEETING NOTES TEMPLATE

Title of Meeting:
Date of Meeting:
Attendees: List of people attending meeting
Absentees: List of people not in attendance

Meeting Agenda:
Item 1—important discussions and decisions made
Item 2
Item 3 (etc.)
Questions and Answers: Take notes on all questions asked and answered during the meeting.
Action Items: Action items, assignments, assignees, and deadlines should be listed here.
Ideas, Questions, and Follow-Ups: This is where you will jot down your questions or follow ups once the meeting has ended.

A COUPLE OF TIPS WHEN WRITING YOUR MEETING NOTES

Which method is best? Pen and Paper or Laptop. The choice is up to you. Laptops are easier to edit and are an easier way to organize your notes but instead of writing notes, one tends to write down words verbatim. Pen and paper tend to make the writer write down key points instead of sentences and make note taking easier and more fluid. Be sure to incorporate your speedwriting skills. And if possible, record your meeting so you can check your facts and quotes if you have questions.

HOW TO TAKE MINUTES DURING A MEETING

Meeting minutes are the notes and documentation taken during a professional or corporate meeting. They are far more detailed and structured than meeting notes. Minutes require a list of the participants as well as a list of those who are absent, the time that the meeting began and the time that it ended, key topics discussed and actions taken and/or decisions made during the meeting.

Meeting minutes, unlike those of meeting notes, are considered to be a form of legal documentation. These documents will ensure the company has an accurate record of past meetings.

PLAN AHEAD

The following are five easy steps on how to write meeting minutes:

Effective meeting notes require some preplanning. While reviewing the meeting agenda, decide which format you will be using for the meeting minutes. You can always refer to the two templates below or develop your own format. Use whichever works best for you as this is going to set you up to transcribe your meeting in an organized manner.

USE THE AGENDA AS A GUIDE

Following the agenda will allow you to outline your minutes prior to the meeting. You can fill in the date and time. If you know who will be attending, you can write their names in. The same goes for those who will be absent. Be sure to document the decisions made concerning previous meetings before you review the meeting agenda. Be sure to stay objective when writing your minutes.

TRANSCRIBING YOUR NOTES

If possible, transcribe your notes as soon as possible. It is easy to forget the discussions, decisions and actions that take place throughout the duration of the meeting.

After you have written the first draft of your minutes you will need to edit them. For others to understand them, they need to be clear, easy to read and to the point. Always attach any documentation that was referred to at the meeting.

DISTRIBUTING THE MINUTES

Before going ahead and distributing your minutes, be sure that they have been reviewed and cleared by supervisors or administrators. There may also be some type of protocol prior to sharing this information.

ALWAYS SAVE YOUR MINUTES

Always file or store your minutes in a safe place as they are considered to be legal documents. Make sure that you can quick reference them when needed.

Below are two sample minutes templates. Choose which one works best for you.

SAMPLE MINUTES TEMPLATE #1

Minutes of the Meeting:_____
Location of Meeting:_____
Present at Meeting:_____
Absent at Meeting:_____
The regular meeting of the _____ of _____was
 called to order on
_____at_____by_____.
 I. Approval of Agenda
The agenda for the meeting was distributed and approved
 II. Review of Previous Minutes
The minutes of the previous meeting were reviewed on_____
 and approved
 III. Consideration and Open Issues
_____

_____

 IV. Agenda and Time of Next Meeting
The next meeting will be held at _____on_____at_____
The agenda for the next meeting is as follows:
_____

_____

The meeting was adjourned at_____
Minutes Submitted by:_____
Minutes approved by:_____

SAMPLE MINUTES TEMPLATE #2

Company/Department Name_____
Date_____

I. Call to order

Facilitator Name called to order the regular meeting of the Organization/Committee Name

II. Roll call

Secretary Name conducts a roll call. The following persons were present: attendee names.

III. Approval of minutes from last meeting

Secretary Name reads the minutes from the last meeting. The minutes were approved as read.

IV. Open Issues
  a) Open issues/summary of discussion
  b) Open issues/summary of discussion
  c) Open issues/summary of discussion

V. New business
  a) New business/summary of discussion
  b) New business/summary of discussion
  c) New business/summary of discussion

VI. Adjournment

Facilitator Name adjourned the meeting at time
Minutes submitted by: Name
Minutes approved by: Name

Chapter 13

Compare, Contrast, and Lists

Your notetaking method or methods will differ depending on the subject matter involving your reading assignment or lecture. Sometimes you're reading or lecture will involve the similarities and differences of people, places, and/or things. This method of notetaking is referred to as compare and contrast.

The word compare means alike and the word contrast means different. Read the paragraph below and look at the example to follow.

JOHNNY AND RICHIE—THE TWINS

Johnny and Richie are similar in some ways, yet, very different in others. Both are 11 years old but Johnny is 6 minutes older than Richie.

The twins are fraternal which means that are not identical in looks. Both have brown hair and light blue eyes.

Johnny likes to read and build things on his computer. Richie would rather play sports. Both boys love to swim. Johnny likes to eat pasta, rice, potatoes, and vegetables. Richie likes to eat meat and potatoes.

Richie is very meticulous about how he dresses. Johnny is less meticulous. Both boys like to ride their bikes and scooters.

Now, with the information you have just read, review the breakdown below and then fill in the contrast and comparison form.

JOHNNY

11 years old
6 minutes older than Richie
Fraternal twin
Light brown hair and light blue eyes
Likes to read and build things on his computer
Likes to swim
Likes to eat pasta, rice, potatoes and vegetables
Less meticulous about how he dresses
Likes to ride his bike and scooter

RICHIE

11 years old
6 minutes younger than Johnny
Fraternal twin
Light brown hair and light blue eyes
Likes to play sports
Likes to swim
Likes to eat meat and potatoes
Very meticulous about how he dresses
Likes to ride his bike and scooter

Using the above lists, show the similarities and differences between Johnny and Richie in the format below:

JOHNNY AND RICHIE

SIMILARITIES	DIFFERENCES

LISTS

This method should be applied when you read or hear a list of ideas or facts. This cue that you will receive from reading the book or listening to the lecturer will be something like this:

There are seven reasons why . . .
There are various ways in which to . . . "T"
There are many different kinds of . . .

Let's look at the example below.

HOLLYWOOD'S MOVIE MESSAGES

"The Hollywood film industry has many ways of sending out messages through its movies to the American public. There are movies that scare us, there are movies that amuse us, there are movies that make us aware of the world around us and there are movies that educate us."

There are four key words in this paragraph. If you know which words these are, then your notes should look like this:

HOLLYWOOD'S MOVIE MESSAGES

| To scare |
| To amuse |
| To make us aware |
| To educate |

We call this a Simple List. You can use this method during a lecture or an assigned reading. Try practicing this method on the passage below. I will give you the first two notes. You do the rest.

THE TEACHINGS OF SCUBA DIVING

Diving can be a remarkable teacher. It teaches self-confidence to the meek, humility to the bold, and philosophy to all. It teaches you to make wise decisions, as well as build character, determination, and judgment. It provides a common sense of responsibility for one another's safety. Last, but not least, it builds strength and endurance to keep you healthy and fit.

NOTES ON THE TEACHINGS OF SCUBA DIVING

1. Self-confidence/meek, humility/bold, philosophy/all
2. Wise decisions

_____
_____
_____
_____
_____

Besides the Simple List there is also a method known as the Chronological List.

CHRONOLOGICAL LIST

A chronological list is a list that is arranged in the order of time, events, procedures and/or directions. For example, how would you know how to make chocolate chip cookies without directions? Would you put the chocolate chips in before the butter and eggs? What about the flour and sugar? Do you mix them separately or together? To answer these questions, you will need a chronological list to do it correctly.

Look at the example below on *How to Make Great Chocolate Chip Cookies*. In order for these cookies to look and taste great, we must do exactly as the recipe says and in the order that it says, that would be chronological order.

HOW TO MAKE GREAT CHOCOLATE CHIP COOKIES

1. Preheat oven to 350 degrees.
2. In one bowl mix 1 cup of softened butter (2 sticks), ¾ cup of granulated sugar, ¾ cup of packed brown sugar, 2 large eggs and 1 teaspoon of vanilla. Set aside.
3. In another bowl mix 2 ¼ cups of flour and 1 teaspoon of baking soda. Gradually add these ingredients to the butter, sugar, eggs and vanilla and blend well.
4. Add one 6-ounce package of semi-sweet chocolate chip morsels and ½ cup of walnuts. Fold into batter.
5. Using a teaspoon, drop cookie dough onto a greased or Teflon cookie sheet 2 inches apart. Bake 10 to 13 minutes or until golden brown. Remove from sheet immediately. Makes 3 dozen cookies.

Using the above recipe as a guide, try practicing the chronological list method using your own personal notetaking system.

1. _____
   _____
2. _____
   _____

3. _____
   _____
4. _____
   _____
5. _____
   _____

The following is a fact list. It is one of the most commonly used forms of notetaking when working with a list of people, places, or things.

I am going to give you some facts about two, large metropolitan cities: San Francisco, California and Los Angeles, California. After you have read the information, I will show you how to take notes (using both methods) on the information that you have just read.

THE CITIES OF SAN FRANCISCO AND LOS ANGELES

Both the city of San Francisco and the city of Los Angeles are large, metropolitan cites in the state of California. San Francisco is in the northern part of the state, while Los Angeles is in the southern part of the state.

San Francisco, the city by the bay, is known for its hills, cable cars, great food, the Golden Gate Bridge, and its beautiful skyline.

Los Angeles, home to Hollywood, the film capital of the world, is known for its movie stars, Disneyland, its great beaches, and beautiful weather. Both cities have great sports teams.

San Francisco is home to the World Series Champions, the San Francisco Giants baseball team and Super Bowl Champions, the San Francisco Forty Niners football team. Los Angeles is home to the World Series Champions, the Los Angeles Dodgers, the NBA Champions, the Los Angeles Lakers basketball team and the Los Angeles Rams football team.

Geographically and culturally, San Francisco and Los Angeles are quite different, yet each has something for everyone.

First, let's start with the Fact List.

THE CITIES OF SAN FRANCISCO
AND LOS ANGELES

San Francisco
Location
Northern California

Famous For
Hills
Cable cars
Great food
Golden Gate Bridge
Beautiful skyline

Sports Teams
S. F. Giants
S. F. Forty Niners

Los Angeles
Location
Southern California

Famous For
Hollywood
Movie stars
Disneyland
Great beaches
Beautiful weather

Sports Teams
L. A. Dodgers
L. A. Rams
L. A. Lakers

Now, using the same formula that I have just used, write down the same information but this time use your personal notetaking system.

Chapter 13

S. F.

L. A.

Chapter 14
Test Yourself!

After a lecture or reading assignment, you may want to check on how much material your brain was able to remember. Here's how to do just that.

Write a summary (a short version) of the material you had recently taken notes on. Your summary should be brief and in your own words, not the author's or speaker's words. It should include all the main facts and ideas expressed, *italicized*, and/or defined by either the author or speaker.

Read the story below about throwing (creating) a clay pot on the wheel.

THROWING A POT ON THE WHEEL

I am going to explain to you how to make, or as ceramists' say, throw a clay pot on the wheel. First, you must knead or roll the clay so that the air bubbles are removed. It must be neither too hard nor too soft.

Form a ball of prepared clay and place it directly on the center of the wheel. With your foot, set the wheel in motion and with pressure from your hands, work the clay ball to the exact center of the wheel. Be sure to keep the clay always wet with water or it will dry out.

Once the ball of clay has been centered perfectly, push both your thumbs into the center and open the ball using your other fingers as a guide. With very little pressure, pull the clay upward so that it rises into a cylinder. Once this has been achieved and you have completed your pot, it's not ready to be removed from the wheel.

To remove the pot from the wheel you will need a wire. Hold the wire tight and slide it under the base toward you. After the pot has been removed from the wheel, slide it gently off onto a board and allow to dry.

Below are some notes about what you have just read.

NOTES

Knead/roll clay—no air bubbles.
Clay should be neither too hard nor too soft.
Form ball and place on center of wheel.
Turn wheel with foot—work ball perfectly to center. Keep clay wet.
Use fingers to guide clay.
Light pressure—pull clay up to cylinder shape.
Use tight wire to remove.
Slide under base toward you.
Gently slide off board.
Dry.

Next, you will read a summary of what you have just read based on the above notes.

SUMMARY

When throwing a pot, you must remember to knead/roll the clay until all the air bubbles are out. Be sure that the clay is neither too hard nor too soft. Make a ball with the clay and place it on the center of the wheel. With your foot, turn the wheel and keep the clay in the center. Also, keep it wet at all times. Open the clay with your thumbs guiding it with your fingers. Pull the clay up into a cylinder. When finished, slide a tight wire underneath the pot to remove it from the wheel. Gently slide the pot onto the board and let dry.

Test Yourself!

Now let's see how well you can do on your own. First, read the following short story on *The Game of Basketball and How It All Started*. Second, take notes in the space provided. Last, use your notes to write your summary—also in the spaces provided. Be sure to use your personal notetaking system.

THE GAME OF BASKETBALL AND HOW IT ALL STARTED

Basketball is American through and through. Dr. James A. Naismith, an instructor at the International YMCA Training School, now Springfield College, invented the game in 1891. He fastened a couple of peach baskets to the gymnasium balcony and drafted basic rules that still are reflected in today's code.

Dr. Naismith's basic principles were that there be a horizontal goal above the heads of the players; that a player could not run with the ball and that personal contact be held to a minimum. These rules still apply today.

Basketball is now played all over the world. It is one of the principal Olympic team sports. The rules have been changed and new playing techniques have been contributed to basketball's spectacular rise in popularity. From a slow-paced game of maneuver and position, it has developed a pattern that features quick movement, shooting from anywhere on the court and rapid-fire scoring. The United States is still one of the, if not *the*, best in the world in team competition.

NOTES

SUMMARY

_____
_____
_____
_____
_____
_____
_____
_____

Read the following passage about the author, Jack London. Use the same method as before—first, take notes then write your summary.

JACK LONDON, AUTHOR (1876–1910)

Born in poverty in San Francisco, Jack London worked for ten cents an hour in a cannery as soon as he graduated from grammar school. By the time he published his first book at the age of twenty-four, he had been a hobo, a longshoreman and a gold prospector in Alaska. He had also been in jail for vagrancy and for speaking at a socialist meeting in California.

London's participation in the gold rush to the Klondike (Alaska) in 1896 paid off but not in gold. He used his experiences as the material for his stories. London soon became one of the most highly paid writers in the United States.

Disciplined to write a thousand words a day, he turned out popular adventure fiction such as the famous story and best-selling novel, *The Call of the Wild.*

NOTES

_____
_____
_____
_____

Test Yourself!   61

_____
_____
_____
_____

SUMMARY

_____
_____
_____
_____
_____
_____
_____
_____

Read the following story about *The Women's Right to Vote: The Nineteenth Amendment*. It is quite long. Take notes and then write your summary. Take your time and read the material carefully. Be sure to incorporate your speedwriting skills.

THE WOMEN'S RIGHT TO VOTE—
THE NINETEENTH AMENDMENT

The Nineteenth Amendment to the U.S. Constitution grants American women the right to vote, a right known as women's suffrage and was ratified on August 18, 1920, ending almost a century of protest.

In 1848, the movement for women's rights at the national level began with the Seneca Falls convention organized by Elizabeth Cady Stanton and Lucretia Mott. Both Stanton and Mott, along with Susan B. Anthony and other activists raised public awareness and lobbied the government to grant women the right to vote. After years of conflict and struggle, the *Suffragettes* emerged victorious with the passage of the Nineteenth Amendment.

America's early history denied women many of the basic rights enjoyed by male citizens. Married women couldn't own property and had no legal claim on any monies they may have earned. Taking care of a household and becoming a mother were the only two important factors in being a woman. Politics was for men only.

In 1869 Elizabeth Cady Stanton and Susan B. Anthony created the National Woman Suffrage Association (NWSA) with hopes of a federal constitutional amendment granting women the right to vote.

That same year abolitionists Lucy Stone and Henry Black formed the American Women Suffrage Association (AWSA). This organization believed that women could be granted the right to vote if an amendment was passed by the individual state constitutions. In 1869 the Wyoming Territory granted all females residents age twenty-one and older the right to vote.

In 1878, the National Women Suffrage Association had collected enough influence to lobby the U.S. Congress for a constitutional amendment. The House of Representatives and the Senate debated the issue. But in 1886, when the proposal finally reached the Senate floor eight years later, it was defeated.

In 1890 both the NWSA and the AWSA merged forming the National American Woman Suffrage Association (NAWSA). The strategy was to lobby for women's voting rights on a state-by-state basis. By 1896 Colorado, Utah, and Idaho adopted amendments to their state constitutions giving women the right to vote.

In 1900 a new leader came upon the scene by the name of Carrie Chapman. She was now the new leader of the NAWSA. Between 1910 and 1918 and under Chapman's leadership, Alaska Territory, Arizona, Arkansas, California, Illinois, Indiana, Kansas, Michigan, Montana, Nebraska, Nevada, New York, North Dakota, Oklahoma, Oregon, South Dakota, and Washington extended to women the right to vote.

In 1913, President Woodrow Wilson did not support the women's movement or their right to vote. But in 1919, Wilson switched sides and supported the women by saying that giving them the right to vote was *essential to the great war on humanity.*

Sadly, the proposed amendment failed in the Senate by two votes.

Test Yourself! 63

On May 21, 1919, House representative James R. Mann, a Republican from Illinois and chairman of the Suffrage Committee, proposed the House resolution to approve the Susan Anthony Amendment granting women the right to vote. The measure passed the House 304–89–42 votes above the required two-thirds majority.

Two weeks later, on June 4, 1919, the Senate passed the Nineteenth Amendment by two votes over its two-thirds required majority, 56–25. The amendment was then sent to the states for ratification.

Within six days of the ratification cycle, Illinois, Michigan, and Wisconsin ratified the amendment followed by Kansas, New York, and Ohio. A total of thirty-five states had approved the amendment by March of 1920. This was just short of the three-fourths required for ratification.

Alabama, Georgia, Louisiana, Maryland, Mississippi, South Carolina, and Virginia were opposed to the amendment. But on August 18, 1920, Tennessee tipped the scales and became the deciding vote for women to finally receive the right to vote. It was a twenty-three-year-old Representative Harry T. Burns, a Republican from McMinn County who cast the deciding vote. The Nineteenth Amendment had been fully ratified.

Since the length of the above story is long, use your computer or a notebook to take *notes* and to write your *summary*.

Speedwriting Dictionary

The following is an alphabetized list of commonly used words and their speedwriting abbreviations. Note that some words will have the same abbreviations, but you should be able to distinguish the meaning of the word through the context of your writing. Below are a few symbols that will be used to designate word endings and beginnings:

ing: .
ment: ___
tion/ion/sion: /
ity: ʌ
nt:)
com: (

A	
ability	abl^
able	abl
about	abt
above	abv/abov
accept	acpt
according	accrd.
account	acc)

across	acros
act	act
action	ac/
activity	actv^
actually	actuly
add	+
address	+res/adrs
administration	admnstra/
admit	admt
adult	adlt
affect	afct
after	aftr
again	agn
against	agnst
age	ag/age
agency	agncy
agent	ag)
ago	ago
agree	agre
agreement	agre ____
ahead	ahed
air	air
algebra	alg
all	al
allow	alow
almost	almst
alone	alon
along	alng
already	alrdy

also	also
although	altho
always	alwys
American	Am/Amer
among	amng
amount	amt/am)
analysis	analsis
and	+/and
animal	anml
another	anothr
answer	answr
any	any
anyone	any1
anything	anyth.
appear	appr
apply	aply
approach	aproch
April	Apr
area	area
argue	argu
arm	arm
around	arond
arrive	arriv
art	art/rt
article	artcl
artist	artst
as	as
Asian	/A/
ask	ask

assume	assum
at	@
attack	attak
attention	attn/
attorney	atrny
audience	audienc
August	Aug
author	athr
authority	athor)
available	avalbl
avoid	avod
away	awy
B	
baby	bby
back	bak/bk
bad	bad
bag	bag
ball	bal
bank	bnk
bar	bar
base	bas
be	b
beat	beat
beautiful	butifl
because	becz
become	bcom
bed	bed
before	bfr

begin	bgn
behavior	bhavr
behind	bhnd
believe	bleve
benefit	bnft
best	bst
better	bttr
between	btw
beyond	bynd
big	big
bill	bill
billion	billn
biology	bio
bit	bit
black	blk
blood	blod
blue	blu
board	bord
body	bdy
book	bk
born	brn
both	both
box	bx
boy	boy
break	brk
bring	brng
brother	bro
budget	bdgt
build	bld

building	bld.
business	bus
but	but
buy	buy/by
by	by
C	
call	cal
camera	cmra
campaign	campgn
can	can/cn
cancer	cncr
candidate	cndate
capital	captl/cap
car	car/cr
card	crd
care	care
career	carer
carry	caru
case	cas
catch	ctch
cause	caus
cell	cel
center	cntr
central	cntrl
century	cntury
certain	crtan
certainly	crtnly
chair	chr/char

challenge	chalng
chance	chnce
change	chng/chang
character	chrctr
charge	chrg
check	checkmark
chemistry	chem
child	chld/child
Chinese	Ch/Chin
choice	choic
choose	chos
church	chrch
citizen	citzn
city	cty
civil	cvl
claim	claim/clam
class	clas
clear	clr
clearly	clrly
close	cls/clos
coach	coch
cold	cld
collection	colc/
college	col/colg
color	clr/colr
come	(/com
commercial	(rse
common	(mon
community	(un^

company	co
compare	(pr
computer	(pt
concern	concrn
condition	cond/
conference	confrnc
Congress	Cong
consider	consdr
consumer	consum
contain	certn
continue	cont
control	cntrl
cost	cost/cst
could	coud
country	cntry
couple	cupl
course	crose
court	cort
cover	cvr
create	creat
crime	crim
cultural	cultrl
culture	cultur
cup	c/cup
current	cur)
customer	custmr
cut	cut/ct
D	
dark	drk

data	date
daughter	dgtr/dgt
day	day
dead	ded/dead
deal	deal
death	dth
debate	dbat
decade	decad
December	Dec
decide	dcide
decision	dec/
deep	deep
defense	defns
degree	dgre
Democrat	Dem
democratic	demcrtc
describe	desc/des
design	desin
despite	despit
detail	detal
develop	dev
die	die/di
difference	difrnce
different	difr)
difficult	diff/difclt
dinner	dnr
direction	dirc/
director	dirctr
discover	dscvr
discuss	dscuss

discussion	discus/
disease	diseas
do	do
doctor	dr
dog	dog
door	dor
down	dwn
draw	draw
dream	drm
drive	driv
drop	drop
drug	drug/drg
during	dur.
E	
each	ea
early	erly
east	e/est
eastern	estrn
easy	ez
eat	eat
economic	ecnomic
economy	econmy
edge	edg
education	educ/
effect	efct
effort	efrt
eight	8
either	ethr

election	elec/
else	els
employee	emplye
end	nd/end
energy	enrgy
English	Eng
enjoy	enjy
enough	enuff
enter	entr/ent
entire	entir
environment	environ ____
especially	esply/esp
establish	est/estblsh
even	evn
evening	evn.
event	evnt
ever	evr/ever
every	evry
everybody	evrybdy
everyone	evry1
everything	everything.
evidence	evdnce
exactly	exctly
example	ex
executive	exectv
exist	exst
expect	expct
experience	exp/expr
expert	exprt

explain	expln
eye	i
F	
face	face
fact	fct
factor	fctr
frail	fral
fall	fall
family	fam/fmly
far	far
fast	fst
father	fathr
fear	fer
February	Feb
federal	fedrl/fed
feel	feel
feeling	feel.
few	few
field	fld
fight	flt/flght
figure	figur
fill	fill
film	film/flm
final	fin/fnl
finally	finly
financial	financl
find	fnd
fine	fine

finger	fngr
finish	fin/fnish
fire	fire
firm	frm
first	1st
fish	fsh
five	5
floor	flor
fly	fly
focus	focs
follow	folow
food	food
foot	ft
for	4
force	forc/4c
foreign	forgn/4in
forget	4gt
form	4m/frm
former	fmr/4mr
forward	4wrd
four	4
free	free/fre
French	Fr
Friday	Fri
friend	frnd
from	fr/frm
front	frnt
full	ful/full
fund	fnd

future	futr
G	
game	gam
garden	grdn
gas	gas/gs
general	gen
generation	genra/
geometry	geo
German	Ger
get	get/gt
girl	grl
give	gv
glass	gls
go	go
goal	gol
good	gd
government	govn____
great	gr/grt
green	grn
ground	grnd
group	grup
grow	gro
growth	groth
guess	gus
gun	gun/gn
guy	guy/gy
H	
hair	har

half	haf/1/2
hang	hng
happen	hapn
happy	hapy
hard	hrd
have	hav
he	he
head	head/hed
health	hlth
hear	hear
heart	hrt
heat	heat
heavy	hevy
help	hlp
her	her
here	here
herself	herslf
high	hi
himself	hmslf
his	his/hs
history	hist
hit	hit
hold	hld
holiday	hol/holdy
home	hm
hope	hop
hospital	hosptl
hot	hot/ht
hotel	hottl
hour	hr

house	hous
how	how
however	howevr
huge	huge
human	humn
hundred	100/hndrd
husband	hsbnd
I	
ice	ice/ic
idea	idea
identify	idntfy
if	if
image	imag
imagine	imagn
impact	impct
important	imp)
improve	imprv
in	in
include	inc
including	inc.
increase	inc/incrs
indeed	inded
indicate	indicat
individual	indv
industry	indstry
information	info
inside	insid
instead	insted

Speedwriting Dictionary

institution	institu/
interest	int/intrst
interesting	int
international	intrna/l
internet	intrnt
interview	intrview
into	into
investment	invst____
involve	involv
issue	isue
it	it
Italian	Ital
item	itm
its	its
itself	itslf
J	
January	Jan
Japanese	Jap/Japnse
job	job
join	join
journalism	jrnlsm
July	Jul
June	June
just	jst
K	
keep	kep/keep
key	ky

keyboard	kybrd
kid	kid/kd
kill	kil
kind	knd
kitchen	ktchn
know	kno
knowledge	knowleg
Korean	Kor
L	
land	lnd
language	lang
large	lrg
last	lst
late	late
later	latr
laugh	laf
law	law
lawyer	lawyr
lay	lay
lead	lead
leader	leadr
learn	lern
least	lst
leave	leav
left	lft
leg	leg
legal	legl
less	-

let	let
letter	ltr
level	lvl
lie	lie
life	life
light	lite
like	like
likely	likly
line	line
list	lst
listen	listn
little	litl
live	liv
lobby	loby
local	locl
long	lng
look	lol
lose	lose
loss	los
lot	lot
love	lov
low	low
M	
machine	machn
magazine	magzn/mag
main	main
maintain	maintn
major	maj

majority	majr^
make	make
man	man
manage	mang
management	mang____
manager	mgr
many	mny
March	Mar
market	mrkt
marriage	marig
material	matrl/mat
matter	matr
May	May
maybe	mayb
me	me
mean	mean
measure	msur
media	mdia
medical	medcl
meet	mt
meeting	mt.
member	membr/mbr
memory	memry
mention	men/
message	mes/mesg
method	metgd
Mexico	Mex
middle	mdl/midl
might	might/migt
military	mil/miltry

million	mil
mind	mind/mnd
minute	min
miss	miss/ms
mission	mis/
modern	modrn
moment	mom)
Monday	Mon
money	$
month	mon
more	more/+
morning	mrng
most	most/mst
mother	mom/mothr
mouth	mth/mouth
move	mov
movement	mov____
movie	movi
Mr.	Mr
Mrs.	Mrs
Ms.	Ms
much	mch
music	musc/music
must	mst/must
my	my
myself	myslf
N	
name	name
nation	na/

national	ma/l
natural	natrl
nature	natur
near	near
nearly	nrly
necessary	nec
need	need
network	netwrk
never	nevr
new	new
news	news
newspaper	nwspapr
next	nxt
nice	nice
night	nght
no	no
none	none
nor	nor
north	n/nrth
northern	nrthrn
not	not
note	note
nothing	noth.
notice	notc
November	Nov
now	now
number	#
O	
occur	occr

October	Oct
of	of
off	off
offer	offr
office	off/office
officer	offcr
official	officl
often	oftn
oh	oh
oil	oil
ok	ok
on	on
once	1se
one	1
only	only
onto	on2
open	opn
operation	opera/
opportunity	opportn^
option	op/
or	or
order	ordr
organization	orgniza/
other	othr
others	othrs
our	R
out	out
outside	outsde
over	ovr
own	own

owner	ownr
P	
page	pg
pain	pain
painting	paint.
paper	papr
parent	prnt
part	part/pt
participant	partcp)
particular	partclar
particularly	prtculry
partner	part/prtnr
party	party/prty
pass	pass
past	past
patient	pa/)
pattern	patrn
pay	pay
peach	pech/peach
people	peopl
per	per
perform	perfum
performance	prfrmanc
perhaps	prhaps
period	prd/perod
person	prsn
personal	prsnl
phone	ph

physical	physcl
pick	pik
picture	pictr/pix
piece	piec
place	pl
plan	pln
plant	pla)
play	play/pla
player	playr
point	pt
police	polic
policy	polcy
political	poltcl
politician	poltcn
politics	poltcs
poor	poor
popular	poplr
population	popul/
position	pos/
positive	postv
possible	poss/posbl
power	powr
practice	prac/pract
prepare	prepr
present	pres)
preside	presid
president	pres/presd)
pressure	presr/presur
pretty	prty

prevent	prv)
price	pric
private	priv
probably	probly
problem	problm
process	proces
produce	produc
product	prodct
production	produc/
profession	prof/profesn
professional	profesnal
professor	profesr
program	prog/progrm
project	projct
property	proprty
protect	protct
protest	protst
prove	prov
provide	provid
public	pub/publc
pull	pull
purpose	purps
push	push
put	put
Q	
quality	qual^
quantity	quant^
queen	queen

question	?
quickly	quikly
quiet	quiet
quite	quite
R	
race	rac/race
radio	rado
raise	rase
rang	rang
range	rng
rate	rt/rate
rather	rathr
reach	rech
read	read
ready	redy
real	real
reality	real
realize	real^
really	realy
reason	resn
receive	recv
recent	rec)
recently	rec)ly
recognize	rec/recog
record	rec
red	red
reduce	reduc
reflect	reflct

region	reg/
relate	relat
relationship	rela/shp
religion	relign
religious	religos
remain	reman
remember	rmembr
remove	remov
report	rep/reprt
represent	represnt/rep
Republican	Rep
require	req
research	resrch
resource	res/resorc
respond	respnd
response	respons
responsibility	respsbil^
rest	rst/rest
result	reslt
return	ret/retrn
reveal	reveal
rich	rich
right	rt
rise	rise
risk	rsk
road	road
rock	roc
role	rol
room	rm

rule	rul
run	rn/run
Russian	Rus
S	
safe	saf
same	same
Saturday	Sat
save	sav
say	say
scene	scen
school	sch/schol
science	sci
scientist	scintst
score	scor
sea	sea
season	seasn
seat	seat
second	2nd
section	sec/
security	secur^
see	see
seek	seek
seem	seem/sm
sell	sel
send	snd
senior	senr
sense	sens
September	Sept

series	series
serious	serius
serve	serv/srv
service	servc
set	set
seven	7
several	sevrl/7vrl
sex	sex
shake	shak
share	shar/shr
she	she
shoot	shoot
short	shrt
shot	sht
should	shod
shoulder	sholdr
show	sho
side	side
sign	sign
significant	sig/sgnfc)
similar	simlar
simple	simpl
simply	smply
since	sin/sinc
sing	sng/sing
singer	sngr
single	sngl
sister	sis
sit	sit

site	site
situation	situa/
six	6
size	sz
skill	skl
skin	skn
small	sm
smile	smil
so	so
social	soc/socl
society	soci^
soldier	soldr
some	some
somebody	somebdy
someone	some1
something	somthng
sometimes	somtims
son	son
song	sng/song
soon	soon/sn
sort	sort/srt
sound	sond
source	sorce
south	s/so
southern	sothrn
space	spac
Spanish	Sp/Span
speak	spk
special	specl

specific	specfic
speech	spech
spend	sspnd
sport	sprt
spring	sprng
staff	staf
stage	stag
stand	stnd
standard	standrd
star	*
start	strt
state	st/stat
statement	stat___
station	sta/
stay	stay
step	step
still	stil
stock	stck/stock
stop	stp/stop
store	stor/store
story	stry
strategy	stratgy
street	st
strong	strng
structure	structr
student	stud)
study	stdy
stuff	stuff
style	styl

subject	sub
success	sucess
successful	sucessfl
such	such
suddenly	sudnly
suffer	suffr
suggest	sug/suggst
summer	sum/summr
Sunday	Sun
support	sup/suprt
sure	sure
surface	surfac
system	systm
T	
table	tbl
take	tak/take
talk	talk
task	tsk
tax	tx
teach	tech
teacher	tchr
team	tm
technology	tecnolgy
television	telev/tv
tell	tell/tl
ten	10
tend	10nd
term	trm

test	tst
than	than/thn
thank	thnk
that	that
the	the
their	their
them	thm
themselves	themslvs
then	then
theory	thery
there	there
these	these
they	thy
thing	th.
third	3rd
this	ths/this
those	thos
though	tho
thought	thoght
thousand	
threat	1000/thou
three	3
through	thru
throughout	thruout
throw	thro
Thursday	Thur
thus	thus
time	time
to	to

today	tody
together	togethr
tonight	tongt/tonite
too	2
top	top
total	totl
tough	tuff
toward	towrd
town	twn/town
trade	trad
traditional	tradi^
training	train.
travel	trvl
treat	tret
treatment	tret___
tree	tree
trial	trial
trip	trp
trouble	trubl
true	tru
truth	truth
try	try
Tuesday	Tues
turn	trn
two	2
type	typ
U	
Ukraine	Ukrn

umbrella	umbrlla
under	undr
understand	undrstnd
unit	un/unit
until	untl
up	up
upon	upon/upn
us	us
use	use
usually	usualy
V	
value	valu
various	varius
very	very/vry
victim	vic/victm
view	view
violence	vilenc
violent	vil)
visit	vis/vist
voice	voc/voice
vote	vote/vot
W	
wait	wait
walk	walk/wlk
wall	wal
want	want
war	war

watch	watch
water	h2o
way	way
we	we
weapon	wepn
wear	wear
Wednesday	Wed
week	wk
weight	wt
well	wel
west	w/wst
western	wstrn
what	what
whatever	whatvr
when	when
where	where/wher
whether	whethr
which	which
while	yl
white	yt
who	who
whole	whol
whom	whom
whose	whos
why	y
wife	wife/wif
will	wil
win	win
wind	wind

window	wndow
wish	wsh
with	with
within	withn
without	withot
woman	wom/womn
wonder	wndr
word	wrd
work	wk
worker	wkr
world	wrld
worry	wory
would	wold
write	writ
writer	writr
wrong	wrng
X	
X-rated	xratd
x-ray	xray/xry
Y	
yard	yd
year	yr
yell	yell/yel
yes	yes
yet	yet/yt
you	u
young	yng

your	yor
yourself	yorslf
youth	yuth
Z	
zebra	zbra
zone	zone
zoo	zoo
zoology	zoolgy

References

History.com Editors, 2010. *The 19th Amendment.* https://www.history.com/topics/womens-history/19th-amendment-1#section_11. Accessed April 8, 2021.

McNamara, Robert, 2020. *The Civil War Year By Year/ The Civil War Transformed into a Great National Struggle.* https://www.thoughtco.com/the-civil-war-year-by-year-1773748. *Thought.co.* Accessed March 25, 2021.

National Geographic Kids, n.d. *Great White Shark Facts.* https://www.natgeokids.com/uk/discover/animals/sea-life/great-white-sharks/. Accessed February 4, 2021.

National Geographic Kids, n.d. *Octopus.* https://kids.nationalgeographic.com/animals/invertebrates/facts/octopus. Accessed February 22, 2021.

About the Author

University of San Francisco graduate and author **Dr. Kristine Setting Clark** was a long-time feature writer for the San Francisco 49ers' and Dallas Cowboys' *Gameday* Magazine. A gifted athlete in her own right, physical education teacher, wife, mother, and later, a high school administrator and college professor, Dr Clark has never let anything stand in the way of her goals; not even a life-threatening bout with Hodgkin's Disease, blindness in both eyes for ten months, and the resulting partial blindness, at age 26. Her passion for life, her incredible optimism, and her drive to live life to the fullest have endeared her to her former students, friends, and to those on whom she's written, including her childhood football hero and close friend, Bob St. Clair, former San Francisco 49er and Pro Football Hall of Fame member.

Besides *Undefeated, Untied, and Uninvited: A Documentary of the 1951 University of San Francisco Dons' Football Team*, she has authored nine other books: *Legends of the Hall: 1950s; Lilly: A Cowboy's Story—The Life of Former Dallas Cowboys and Hall of Fame Member, Bob Lilly* (foreword by Roger Staubach), *Tittle: Nothing Comes Easy—The Life of Former Football Great and Hall of Fame Member, Y. A. Tittle* (foreword by Frank Gifford), *The Fire Within—The Life of Former Green Bay Packer and Hall of Fame Member, Jim Taylor* (foreword by Bart Starr).

Released in July 2014 is her book *The Fighting Donovans—A Family History of World Boxing Champion and Hall of Fame Boxer, Mike Donovan, World Champion Boxing Referee and Boxing Hall of Fame*

About the Author

Referee Arthur Donovan, Sr. and Former Baltimore Colt Defensive Tackle and Pro Football Hall of Fame Member, Arthur Donovan, Jr. (forewords by Gino Marchetti and Frank Stallone).

In September 2015 her book *Cheating Is Encouraged!* with former Oakland Raider tight end Mike Siani was released through Skyhorse Publishing (an imprint of W. W. Norton in New York) and in March 2016 her book entitled *Football's Fabulous Fifties—When Men Were Men and the Grass Was Still Real,* was released by St. Johann's Press.

In March 2016 her *Simply English* 3-book curriculum for English As a Second Language and Special Education students was published by Rowman and Littlefield. The following year her *Eight Parts of Speech* book was released, again, by Rowman and Littlefield. In 2019 her latest book, *Sports For All Intramural Sports Program* was released in October (Rowman and Littlefield).

In April 2021 Kristine took a different route and wrote an educational book for children entitled *Callie the Calico Cat & Friends: Callie's Favorite Seasons and American Holidays.* This book is an educational children's story on teaching your child the four seasons and the American holidays. Beautifully illustrated, follow Callie and her friends as they celebrate and teach your child about the beauty of the seasons and our traditional holidays through customs, culture, and fun.

Over the years, Kristine has also held a number of book signing events with the many celebrities from her books at the Pro Football Hall of Fame in Canton, Ohio. She has also been a keynote speaker for many corporate, sports, and educational venues.

Dr. Clark's personality, close relationships with the subjects of her books, and engaging writing style allow her to reach the subject matter on a deeper level, taking the reader to otherwise unavailable territory: the sometimes humorous, always intriguing backstory of the famous events and players in the world of sports. In addition, her achievements have led to an offer to host a sports talk radio show and invitations as a keynote speaker for many corporate, sports, and educational venues.

In 1977 Kristine was diagnosed with Stage IV Hodgkin's Disease and was given three months to live. She eventually beat the disease after enduring ten months of blindness caused by the grueling chemotherapy treatments. In December 2015 she wrote her memoir entitled *Death Was Never an Option! A Humorously Serious Story on Defeating Cancer and Blindness.*

In February 2015 ESPN produced a documentary entitled *The '51 Dons* which was narrated by Johnny Mathis and based on her first book, *Undefeated, Untied and Uninvited: A Documentary of the 1951 University of San Francisco Dons Football Team.*

Dr. Clark resides in Stockton, California, and has two grown children and four grandsons. Her oldest grandson, Justin, is the godson of former 49er All-Pro and Hall of Fame member Bob St. Clair.

www.ingramcontent.com/pod-product-compliance
Lightning Source LLC
Chambersburg PA
CBHW032029230426
43671CB00005B/255